Critical Thinking Activities

Brain Teasers

Grade 3

Author:

Carol Eichel

Illustrator:
Larry Bauer

Editor:
Dona Herweck Rice

Editor-in-Chief:
Sharon Coan, M.S. Ed.

Editorial Project Manager:
Evan D. Forbes, M.S. Ed.

Art Director:
Elayne Roberts

Cover Artist:
Keith Vasconcelles

Product Manager:
Phil Garcia

Imaging:
Hillary Merriman

Publishers:
Rachelle Cracchiolo, M.S. Ed.
Mary Dupuy Smith, M.S. Ed.

Teacher Created Materials, Inc.
P.O. Box 1040
Huntington Beach, CA 92647
©1995 Teacher Created Materials, Inc.
Made in U.S.A.
ISBN-1-55734-488-4

TABLE OF CONTENTS

INTRODUCTION

Brain Teasers provides ways to exercise and develop brain power! Each page stands alone and can be used as a quick and easy filler activity. The pages can be distributed to students as individual worksheets or made into transparencies for presentation to the entire class at once. The book is divided into sections so the teacher can find activities related to a subject being taught or to a particular student's needs. The activities are especially useful in helping students develop:

- Logic and other critical thinking skills.

- Creative thinking skills.

- Research skills.

- Spelling skills.

- General vocabulary skills.

- General knowledge skills.

FAMOUS PAIRS

Name the famous partners.

Ren and _____

Hansel and _____

Superman and _____

_____ and the Beast

_____ and Robin

_____ and Minnie

Barbie and _____

Orville and _____

Popeye and _____

_____ and Miss Piggy

_____ and Judy

_____ and Mr. Hyde

Jack and _____

Lady and _____

Bert and _____

PICK A PAIR

List items that are sold in pairs.

THINGS WITH HOLES

Brainstorm a list of things with holes. Can you think of at least twenty?

_____   _____

_____   _____

_____   _____

_____   _____

_____   _____

_____   _____

_____   _____

_____   _____

_____   _____

_____   _____

_____   _____

_____   _____

NAME THREE OF EACH

Write three words that belong in each category named below.

1. Things on your face _____

2. Things that come in pairs _____

3. Things found in your mom's purse _____

4. Palindromes _____

5. Things that float _____

6. Fairy tale characters _____

7. Sports _____

8. Vegetables _____

9. Things with stripes _____

10. Authors _____

11. Toys _____

12. Things to keep you warm _____

13. Colors _____

14. Kinds of dogs _____

15. Places people live _____

16. Bodies of water _____

17. Snack foods _____

18. Farm animals _____

    6

THOSE FAMOUS THREES

Name each of the following threesomes.

1. The first three U.S. presidents to live in the White House

   _____   _____   _____

2. The three presidential memorials in Washington, D.C.

   _____   _____   _____

3. Dorothy's and Toto's three travelling companions to Oz

   _____   _____   _____

4. The Three Bears

   _____   _____   _____

5. the three basic primary colors

   _____   _____   _____

6. The three good fairies in the animated film, *Sleeping Beauty*

   _____   _____   _____

7. The three men in the tub

   _____   _____   _____

8. The three Wise Men

   _____   _____   _____

9. The three R's

   _____   _____   _____

10. Donald Duck's nephews

   _____   _____   _____

11. The Three Stooges

   _____   _____   _____

12. The three wise monkeys

   _____   _____   _____

ALL ALIKE

Read the words on each line. Explain how they are alike. An example has been done for you.

Duck, chicken, goose = poultry

1. East, west, south _____

2. Niece, daughter, grandma _____

3. One, nine, fifteen _____

4. Gorgeous, glamorous, beautiful _____

5. North America, South America, Australia _____

6. April, November, June _____

7. California, Illinois, Georgia _____

8. Armstrong, Aldrin, Loveall _____

9. Phil, Paul, Peter _____

10. Saturn, Jupiter, Earth _____

11. Rose, carnation, peony _____

12. Triangle, tripod, tricycle _____

13. Sneezy, Doc, Grumpy _____

14. Red, yellow, blue _____

15. Almanac, thesaurus, dictionary _____

WORD PAIRS

Write the missing half of each word pair.

1. hot and _____

2. lock and _____

3. black and _____

4. body and _____

5. scream and _____

6. left and _____

7. bacon and _____

8. cat and _____

9. up and _____

10. burgers and _____

11. peace and _____

12. thunder and _____

13. back and _____

14. thick and _____

15. tooth and _____

16. sticks and _____

17. aches and _____

18. bread and _____

19. hammer and _____

20. hide and _____

A VISIT TO THE ZOO

Laura, Phil, Jane, and Mike recently visited the St. Louis Zoo to see their favorite animals. One liked koalas, another liked zebras, a third liked monkeys, and a fourth liked giraffes. While at the zoo, each person ate one of the following: a corndog, a hot dog, hamburger, or popcorn. Using the clues below, determine each person's favorite animal and what he or she had to eat. Mark an X in each correct box.

1. The girls like the koalas and giraffes while the boys like the zebras and monkeys.

2. Mike ate his food on a stick while Laura ate hers on a bun.

3. Laura's favorite animal originates in Australia.

4. The boy who loves the zebras also loves hot dogs.

	koala	zebra	monkey	giraffe	hamburger	corn dog	hot dog	popcorn
Laura								
Phil								
Jane								
Mike								

BIRTHDAY PARTIES

Eight children, including Sarah, will all turn ten years of age this year. From the clues given, determine the month of each child's birth. Mark an X in each correct box.

1. A common holiday is celebrated on Jill's birthday.

2. Andrea's birthday is before Jeff's but after Millie's and Sarah's.

3. Sarah's birthday is exactly one month after Millie's.

4. Andrew's birthday is during the winter months.

5. Max's birthday comes after Andrea's but before Jeff's.

	Feb. 15	Mar. 24	April 1	May 1	July 10	Sept. 9	Oct. 15	Dec. 25
Andrea								
Andrew								
Sarah								
Sam								
Jill								
Jeff								
Millie								
Max								

PRACTICE MAKES PERFECT

Nicole, Sean, Justin, and Janis are taking music lessons from Mrs. Reatherford. Each student is learning to play one of the following instruments: piano, flute, drums, or clarinet. Mrs. Reatherford asks that each of her students practice for at least thirty minutes per evening. Find out from the clues below what instrument is being played by which student and for how long each evening. Mark an X in each correct box.

1. Nicole practices longer than Sean but less than Janis.

2. Janis does not play the drums or flute, but Sean plays one of them.

3. Justin plays the clarinet and practices for more than 30 minutes.

4. The person who practices 45 minutes plays the piano and the person who plays the clarinet practices less than the person who is taking flute lessons.

	Piano	Drums	Flute	Clarinet	30 min.	35 min.	40 min.	45 min.
Nicole								
Sean								
Justin								
Janis								

SPORTS NUTS

Matt, Brian, Jon, Neil, and Jason each love sports, but each loves to play one particular sport most of all. From the three clues given, determine which sport each boy loves to play the most. Mark an X in each correct box.

1. Matt loves baseball or hockey, Jon loves basketball or soccer, and Neil's favorite sport is not soccer or basketball.

2. Jason's favorite sport is played on the ice.

3. Brian's sport is played on a court and he hopes to become as well-known as his favorite player, Michael Jordan.

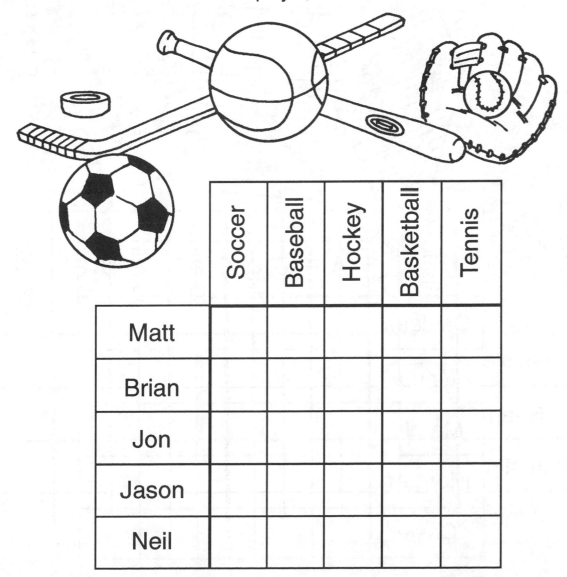

	Soccer	Baseball	Hockey	Basketball	Tennis
Matt					
Brian					
Jon					
Jason					
Neil					

EXAM TIME

As Mrs. Myers prepared to pass back the last math exam, five anxious students awaited their grades. Using the clues below, determine each child's grade. Mark an X in each correct box.

1. Chelsea, who did not get an A on her test, scored higher than Morgan and Linda.

2. Marcia and Linda both scored higher than Casie.

3. Morgan received a C on her test.

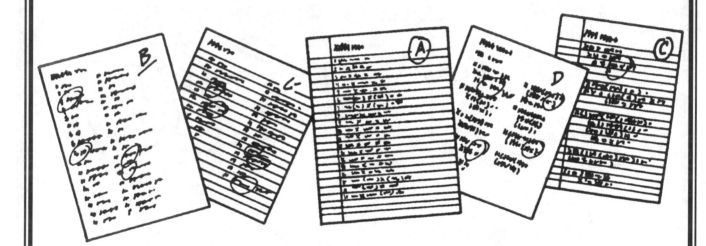

	A	B	C	C –	D
Chelsea					
Linda					
Marcia					
Morgan					
Casie					

WHO'S WHO?

Mr. Fitzpatrick has three boys in his class who go by variations of the name Andrew. From the statements below, determine each boy's full name and age. Mark an X in each correct box.

1. Jones is younger than Andrew but older than Smith.

2. Andy is not the youngest.

	Smith	Jones	Rogers	8	9	10
A. J.						
Andy						
Andrew						

BLACK OUT

Black out every letter that appears four or more times. The letters that are left will spell out the answer to the following riddle:

What is an unusually small skunk called? _____

B	D	P	F	E	G	T	I	X	I	C	L	O
L	P	V	B	L	O	X	A	G	P	W	M	T
F	J	E	T	X	C	W	X	B	I	P	L	O
W	O	D	I	L	M	F	P	V	E	J	W	I
M	S	C	H	X	R	W	U	B	N	M	K	T
F	O	G	E	T	J	D	O	L	V	G	P	C
D	I	G	B	L	X	M	I	C	E	F	W	J
J	T	V	E	T	O	F	G	L	P	J	M	V
F	O	C	D	S	G	K	B	U	E	N	L	K
P	O	G	F	X	I	L	V	T	M	J	E	T
L	X	M	B	W	V	E	T	O	L	M	V	G
Y	W	O	D	T	L	V	B	O	X	Z	I	P

SPECIAL DAYS OF THE MONTH

The following puzzle contains the names of 16 special days that are celebrated throughout the year from New Year's Day through Christmas. Can you find all 16?

```
H E Q S L A B O R D A Y G X F V N L
A M C H R I S T M A S F T W O I A I
L D V Z Y U M M L B L B K H U S P N
L W V E T E R A N S D A Y S R T R C
O E P M E M O R I A L D A Y T P I O
W A S L I N C T L N O I R T H A L L
E S N T B E F I N P E I H L O T F N
E T W F D A C N T G D D C E F R O S
N E N H R R A L W M C G E Y J I O B
I R E A U S O K I O A Z L K U C L I
K V A L E N T I N E S D A Y L K S R
M R Q C S C O N L L C L V D Y S D T
U E X R I A C G X B Q B R H E D A H
M O T H E R S D A Y E U H S Y A Y D
O B N E W Y E A R S D A Y O F Y U A
B T K A U K O Y F A T H E R S D A Y
G J G F C O L U M B U S D A Y H Y O
```

MONTHS OF THE YEAR AND DAYS OF THE WEEK

Find all the months and days hidden in the puzzle below.

```
A  P  R  I  L  H  F  R  I  D  A  Y  E
U  U  O  C  T  O  B  E  R  E  S  N  O
G  U  Z  B  H  M  T  J  J  X  U  S  L
U  F  K  C  U  A  C  T  T  J  N  A  S
S  S  R  H  R  Y  C  U  I  D  D  T  E
T  A  O  I  S  F  Y  E  P  J  A  U  P
M  F  W  E  D  N  E  S  D  A  Y  R  T
M  O  N  D  A  Y  R  D  E  N  B  D  E
J  U  L  Y  Y  T  J  A  M  U  L  A  M
F  E  B  R  U  A  R  Y  K  A  T  Y  B
D  D  E  C  E  M  B  E  R  R  R  R  E  E
N  O  V  E  M  B  E  R  O  Y  M  N  R
M  E  R  C  H  F  E  B  U  A  R  Y  L
```

18

COLOR THIS DESIGN

Color this design so that no shapes of the same color touch one another. You may use only three colors. (Hint: Think out the design before you begin to color.)

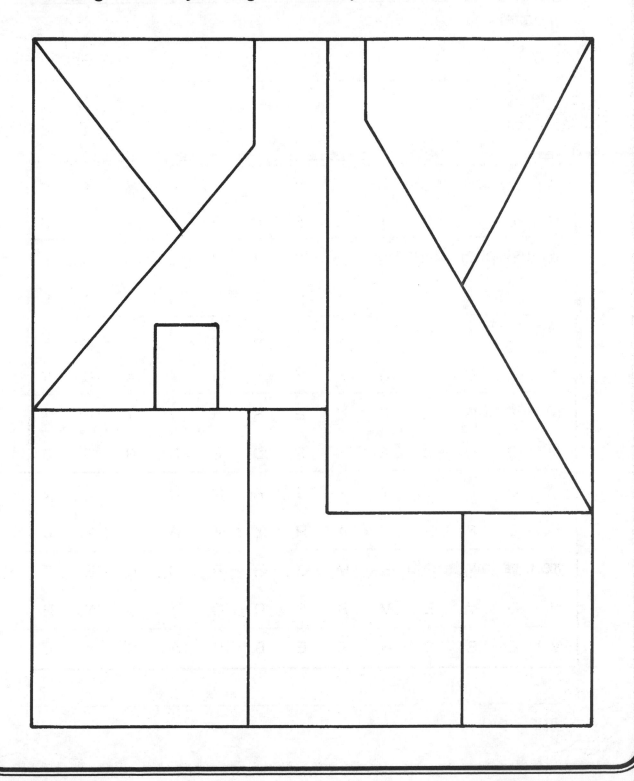

WHAT'S THE QUESTION?

Write an appropriate question for each of the following answers.

1. _____

   Jupiter

2. _____

   Hawaii

3. _____

   yes

4. _____

   Christopher Columbus

5. _____

   13

6. _____

   hexagon

7. _____

   no

8. _____

   red, yellow, and blue

9. _____

   50

10. _____

    apple pie

GET TO KNOW YOUR CLASSMATES

Fill each blank with the name of a classmate who fits the description. Use each person's name only once. Do not forget to include yourself.

1. _____ has ridden a horse.

2. _____ lives on a farm.

3. _____ has green eyes.

4. _____ has been to Washington, D.C.

5. _____ has taken ballet.

6. _____ is left-handed.

7. _____ has a sibling under one year of age.

8. _____ wears glasses.

9. _____ plays ice hockey.

10. _____ has a home computer.

11. _____ collects stamps.

12. _____ likes to go fishing.

13. _____ has a pet turtle.

14. _____ was born outside the state.

15. _____ loves to read.

16. _____ has visited Disney World.

17. _____ rides a bike to school.

18. _____ collects baseball cards.

19. _____ had all A's on a report card once.

20. _____ has grandparents in another state.

COMPLETE THE PHRASE

Complete each of the following phrases with the first thing that comes to mind.

1. I like to eat at _____

2. If I were the teacher, I would _____

3. I like people who _____

4. I am happy when _____

5. In my free time, I like to _____

6. I am really good at _____

7. It bothers me when _____

8. My mother is _____

9. It hurts when _____

10. I never want to forget _____

11. Five years from now, I will _____

12. If I could call one person, I would call _____

13. I feel sorry for _____

14. In the rain, I can _____

15. What I want most in the world is _____

16. My father is _____

17. My favorite season is _____

18. My favorite book is _____

19. My favorite person is _____

20. The best thing about me is _____

HIDDEN MEANINGS

Figure out the meaning of each box below.

Open	**ARREST** <u> </u> **YOU'RE**	D O DOUBLE B L E
1._____	2. _____	3. _____
<u>**Stand**</u> I	1	
4._____	5. _____	6. _____
	cycle cycle cycle	NOON GOOD
7._____	8. _____	9. _____
MAC	chair	T O U C H
10._____	11. _____	12. _____

MORE HIDDEN MEANINGS

Figure out the meaning of each box below.

Jack	Tim	**DICE DICE**

1. _____   2. _____   3. _____

wear ――― **long**	r/e/a/d/i/n/g	**get**

4. _____   5. _____   6. _____

TI*JUST*ME	**GI** ――― **CCCCC**	*GOING* DIET

7. _____   8. _____   9. _____

SAND	T O W N	**mmoaonn**

10. _____   11. _____   12. _____

ADDITION AND SUBTRACTION

Place + and − signs between the digits so that both sides of each equation are equal.

1. 6   4   1   2   6   2   =   15

2. 9   1   3   1   4   1   =   5

3. 9   3   4   1   2   3   =   14

4. 5   1   1   3   4   6   =   18

5. 9   8   6   3   5   3   =   8

6. 2   1   8   9   3   5   =   20

7. 5   3   2   4   1   5   =   12

8. 4   9   3   7   3   1   =   11

9. 7   6   2   8   7   1   =   3

10. 9   9   9   2   2   8   =   1

NAMES AND NUMBERS

1. Name the five senses.

   _____

2. Name the Three Bears.

   _____

3. Name the seven colors of the rainbow.

   _____

4. Name the three R's.

   _____

5. Name Santa's nine reindeer.

   _____

6. Name the five Great Lakes.

   _____

7. Name the four months with thirty days.

   _____

8. Name the three basic primary colors.

   _____

9. Name the two colors of the Canadian flag.

   _____

10. Name the seven dwarfs in Disney's *Snow White and the Seven Dwarfs*.

    _____

    _____

CHANGE FOR FIFTY CENTS

There are over 75 ways to make change for 50 cents. Work with a friend to list as many ways as you can. List the coins in order on each line, from largest to smallest. (Hint: Working from large to small coins will also help you find more ways to make change.) The list has been started for you. If you need more space, continue your list on the back of this paper.

Use the following abbreviations:

hd (half dollar)   **q** (quarter)   **d** (dime)   **n** (nickel)   **p** (penny)

1. 1 hd

2. 2 q

3. _____

4. _____

5. _____

6. _____

7. _____

8. _____

9. _____

10. _____

11. _____

12. _____

13. _____

14. _____

15. _____

TIMELY CHORE

Each word in the time box refers to a specific time span. List the words in order from the shortest time span to the longest. Then, explain how long each time span is.

	Time Span	How Long Is It?
1.		
2.		
3.		
4.		
5.		
6.		
7.		
8.		
9.		
10.		
11.		
12.		

Time Box

second	hour	millennium
fortnight	day	month
minute	score	century
year	decade	week

CALCULATOR FUN

Answer each math problem with a calculator. When you have the answer, turn the calculator upside-down to find an answer for each of the clues in parentheses. The first one is done for you.

1. (Too big) 21,000 + 14,001 = <u>35,001 (loose)</u>

2. (A sphere) 21,553 + 16,523 = _____

3. (Make honey) 10,000 - 4662 = _____

4. (Petroleum) 142 x 5 = _____

5. (Tool for watering the garden) 7008 ÷ 2 = _____

6. (Not feeling well) 348 + 424 - 1 = _____

7. (To cry) 0.02004 + 0.02004 = _____

8. (Boy's name) 9376 - 1658 = _____

9. (City in Idaho) 27413 + 7695 = _____

10. (Antonym for "tiny") 206 + 206 + 206 = _____

EQUATIONS

Each equation below contains the initials of words that will make it complete. Find the missing words. An example has been done for you.

2,000 P in a T = 2,000 pounds in a ton

1. 7 D in SW =_____

2. 9 P on a BT = _____

3. 5 L in the GL = _____

4. 60 S in a M = _____

5. 12 I in a F =_____

6. 32 T in an A = _____

7. 7 D in a W = _____

8. 3 S in a T =_____

9. 7 C on the E =_____

10. 12 M in a Y = _____

11. 9 P in the SS = _____

12. 100 P in a D =_____

13. 11 P on a FT = _____

14. 24 H in a D = _____

15. 12 E in a D = _____

16. 4 S in a Y =_____

17. 50 S in the US = _____

18. 3 PC =_____

19. 13 S on the USF = _____

20. 7 C in the R = _____

WHICH IS IT?

Circle the correct number for each item.

1.	Sides on a rectangle	3	4	5
2.	Years in a century	25	50	100
3.	Horns on a triceratops	1	2	3
4.	Years in a decade	10	20	100
5.	Days in a year	360	365	367
6.	Dwarfs in *Snow White*	5	7	9
7.	Number in a dozen	10	12	13
8.	Sides on a die	4	5	6
9.	States in the United States	13	48	50
10.	Rings of the Olympic symbol	5	6	7
11.	Points on a snowflake	4	5	6
12.	Number that makes a palindrome	121	309	6761
13.	Squares on a checkerboard	64	66	88
14.	Legs on an insect	4	6	8
15.	Hours in a day	24	30	60

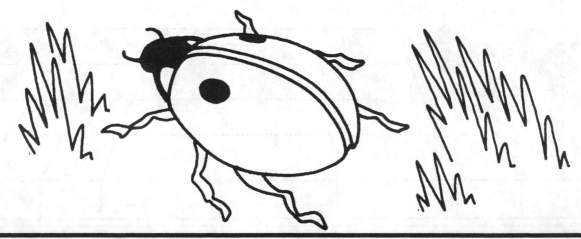

HOW MANY?

Answer each question with a number.

1. How many planets in our solar system have no moon?_____

2. How many sense organs does a person have? _____

3. How many stars are on the U.S. flag? _____

4. How many cardinal directions are on a map? _____

5. How many keys are on a piano? _____

6. How many rings are on the Olympic flag? _____

7. How many Great Lakes are there?_____

8. How many voices are in a trio? _____

9. How many colors are in a rainbow? _____

10. How many days of Christmas are there in the song?_____

11. How many maple leaves are on the Canadian flag? _____

12. How many planets are in our solar system? _____

13. How many squares are on a checkerboard? _____

14. How many years are in a century? _____

15. How many books are in the *Bible?*_____

TRUE OR FALSE

Before each of the following statements, circle T if the statement is true and F if the statement is false. Be prepared to explain any "false" responses.

1. T F Washington Monument is in Washington, D.C.

2. T F A telescope is used to view things that are far away.

3. T F Three is an even number.

4. T F The Pacific Ocean is on the east coast of North America.

5. T F A hexagon has fewer sides that an octagon.

6. T F There are 12 months in every Gregorian year.

7. T F The color red is a primary color.

8. T F Lincoln was the third president of the United States.

9. T F Half-past-eight is the same as 8:30.

10. T F Thanksgiving comes before Labor Day.

11. T F Pierre Trudeau is the Prime Minister of Canada.

12. T F All insects have 6 legs.

13. T F Australia is an island continent.

14. T F Happy and merry are synonyms.

15. T F In Roman numerals, IX is 11.

16. T F A triangle has four sides.

17. T F The U.S. is north of Canada.

18. T F The fourth letter of the alphabet is "D."

DO YOU KNOW?

1. When a car has 2 license plates (one in the front and one in the rear), which plate gets the yearly registration sticker?

   _____

2. How many books are in the Old Testament of the *Bible*? _____

3. Are there more red or white stripes on the U.S. flag? _____

4. From west to east, name the second president carved on Mt. Rushmore. _____

5. On the count in baseball, is the first number strikes or balls?

   _____

6. The Statue of Liberty holds her torch in which hand? _____

7. Does an insect have 6 or 8 legs? _____

8. Are there 60, 90, or 180 degrees in a right angle?_____

9. How many numbers are in a zip code? _____

10. In *A Visit from Saint Nicholas*, how many reindeer pull Santa's sleigh?_____

11. In a fraction, what is the bottom number called?

    _____

12. Which season comes after summer? _____

13. On which side of the horse do you mount and dismount?

    _____

14. Which is more, minimum or maximum? _____

34

TRUE OR FALSE

1. T F Sir Isaac Newton discovered gravity by watching an apple fall.

2. T F The longest river in the world is the Mississippi River.

3. T F The smallest bird in the world is the hummingbird.

4. T F The moon gives off its own light.

5. T F All dinosaurs were carnivores.

6. T F The fastest land animal is the African cheetah.

7. T F Spiders have six legs.

8. T F Synonyms are words that mean the same or nearly the same.

9. T F There are over 100 planets in our solar system.

10. T F Grownups have a total of 32 permanent teeth.

11. T F The first person to walk on the moon was Neil Armstrong.

12. T F Whales can stay under water for more than an hour.

13. T F The capital of Illinois is Chicago.

14. T F Vaccinations protect you from getting diseases.

15. T F Every time you blink, you are actually crying.

16. T F A baby goat is called a kid.

17. T F Abraham Lincoln is pictured on a quarter.

18. T F An attic is below a house.

ENGLISH LANGUAGE TRIVIA

1. What are the two main parts of a sentence? _____

2. What punctuation mark is used in a contraction? _____

3. What words name a person, place, thing, or idea? _____

4. What do we call stories that are made up rather than true?

   _____

5. In the book *Charlotte's Web,* what is the rat's name?

   _____

6. In an address, what punctuation mark comes between the city and state? _____

7. What do we call a statement that tells what a person thinks or believes? _____

8. In a friendly letter, what punctuation mark is placed after the greeting? _____

9. Give the contraction for *will no*t. _____

10. What is the mini-dictionary in the back of some textbooks called?_____

11. What is the plural of sheep? _____

    _____

12. Do antonyms mean the same or opposite as one another?

    _____

13. In the dictionary, which comes first, maybe or maypole? _____

14. What type of story has a moral at the end? _____

15. What Japanese poetry follows a pattern of 5-7-5 syllables?

    _____

SCIENCE TRIVIA

1. What instrument is used to measure temperature?

_____

2. What are animals without backbones called?_____

3. With what does a fish breathe? _____

4. In what sea creatures are pearls found? _____

5. What instrument is used to view things that are far away?

_____

6. Which is the sixth planet from the sun? _____

7. What animal uses its odor as a weapon? _____

8. How many legs does a spider have? _____

9. What birds can fly backwards? _____

10. What is another name for very low clouds? _____

11. What is a frog called when it still has gills? _____

12. Which mammals can fly? _____

13. What is a group of fish called? _____

14. What is another name for a mushroom? _____

15. What do we call the ends of a magnet? _____

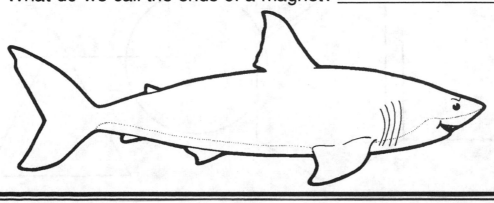

MATH TRIVIA

1. How many minutes in 2 hours? _____

2. How many dimes are in a dollar? _____

3. What is a 3-sided figure called? _____

4. What does a sundial do? _____

5. Two tons is equal to how many pounds? _____

6. What mark separates the hour and the minutes when one is writing down time? _____

7. How many items in a dozen? _____

8. How many sides does a hexagon have? _____

9. What do you call the result of adding two numbers? _____

10. How many centimeters are in a meter? _____

11. How many months are in half of a year? _____

12. Which plane figure has 8 sides?_____

13. How many sides are there on a die? _____

14. How many years are in a decade? _____

15. How many hours are in a day? _____

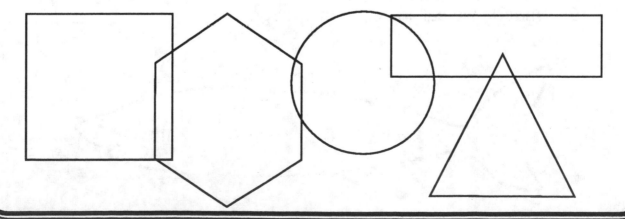

SOCIAL STUDIES TRIVIA

1. On which continent is Canada located? _____

2. In traveling north, what direction is to the right?_____

3. On the American flag, are there more red or white stripes?

    _____

4. What is the longest river in the U.S.? _____

5. What does "N" on a map normally represent? _____

6. Who invented the telephone? _____

7. What is a book of maps called? _____

8. Name the highest mountain in the world.

    _____

9. What do you call a piece of land surrounded with water on all
   sides? _____

10. What are the names of the three ships Columbus took on his
    famous journey? _____

11. On what mountain are four famous presidents' faces carved?

    _____

12. Name the five Great Lakes. _____

    _____

13. Of England, Australia, Peru, and Canada, which nation does not
    have English as a national language? _____

14. Name the ocean west of North America. _____

15. What is the capital of Hawaii?_____

GENERAL TRIVIA

1. How many sides does a snowflake have? _____

2. Whose picture is on the American penny? _____

3. What is another name for a bison? _____

4. What two primary colors are mixed to make orange?

   _____

5. Which bird is known for its beautiful tail? _____

6. What is the commander of a ship called? _____

7. What is another name for the season of fall? _____

8. From what animal do we get wool? _____

9. Which of the seven dwarfs never speaks? _____

10. In *The Wizard of Oz*, what color is the brick road? _____

11. What is a person wearing if he has on spectacles? _____

12. What relationship is your father's brother to you?

    _____

13. What is the art of Japanese paper folding called?

    _____

14. What is a baby kangaroo called? _____

15. What color is the filling in an Oreo cookie? _____

RHYMING WORD PAIRS

Find an adjective that rhymes with a noun so that, together, the two words have about the same meaning as the phrase that is given. An example has been done for you.

girl from Switzerland = Swiss miss

1. ailing William _____

2. mischievous boy _____

3. unhappy friend _____

4. bashful insect _____

5. comical rabbit _____

6. overweight referee _____

7. obese feline _____

8. unhappy father _____

9. soaked dog _____

10. watered-down red juice _____

11. large swine _____

12. flower that hates to work _____

13. tiny bug _____

14. ill hen _____

15. overweight rodent _____

SCHOOL DAYS

Acrostics are word puzzles or poems in which the first or last letters of each line form a word or words. In the example below, the first letters of each line form the words "school days." Complete the acrostic by writing a phrase or sentence on each line that begins with the letter given and relates to the subject "school days."

S _____

C _____

H _____

O _____

O _____

L _____

D _____

A _____

Y _____

S _____

ABBREVIATIONS

Write the meaning of each abbreviation.

1. N _____

2. St. _____

3. RR _____

4. S.A. _____

5. M.C. _____

6. C.O.D. _____

7. Wed. _____

8. A.M. _____

9. chap. _____

10. doz. _____

11. qt. _____

12. pkg. _____

13. max. _____

14. Ave. _____

15. Sept. _____

16. yr. _____

17. bldg. _____

18. no. _____

19. temp. _____

20. P.O. _____

A PILE OF GOLD

Use the clues to help you fill in the blanks and circles. Only the circled letters change from one word to the next. The first two have been done for you.

1. Bright-yellow precious metal   (g)   o   l   d

2. Without fear   (b)   o   l   d

3. A sliding fastening for a door

4. A young horse

5. Shed the skin, hair, or shell

6. A small underground animal

7. An open place

8. Grasp and keep

9. A fungus

10. Calm, warm, temperate

11. Not tamed

12. To wither

13. The desire to do something

14. Side of a room

15. A round, bouncing toy

16. Speak or say in a loud voice

17. Trip

18. To load with room for nothing more

19. Drawer for keeping papers in order

20. Heap up or stack

THE STATUE OF LIBERTY

Use the clues below to fill the blanks.

1. ___ ___ T ___ ___   To wash

2. H ___ ___ ___ ___   Glad, pleased, contented

3. E ___ ___ ___ ___   Antonym for late

4. ___ ___ ___ S ___   A four legged animal

5. ___ ___ T ___ ___   Engine for a car

6. ___ ___ A ___   A small open vessel

7. ___ ___ ___ T ___ ___ ___ ___ ___   At once

8. ___ U ___ ___   A male deer

9. ___ ___ ___ E ___ ___ ___   To let go

10. ___ ___ O ___ ___   A sphere, the world

11. F ___ ___ ___ ___   A violent struggle

12. L ___ ___ ___ ___ ___ ___   Suitcases

13. ___ ___ ___ I ___ ___   To wish earnestly for

14. ___ ___ ___ B ___ ___ ___   Join two or more things together

15. ___ E ___ ___   Nuisance

16. ___ R ___ ___   A large black bird

17. ___ ___ T ___ ___ ___   A criminal

18. ___ ___ ___ Y   The seventh month of the year

Challenge: What does the Statue of Liberty have to do with this page?

WORD CHAIN

Use the last two letters of the previous words in the word chain to begin the next word. Continue throughout the chain. The first two have been done for you.

1. To bite repeatedly   ch<u>ew</u>

2. A female sheep   <u>ew</u>e

3. An undesirable in the garden _____

4. Wholesome to eat _____

5. A character in the alphabet _____

6. To rub out _____

7. A division of the year _____

8. One time _____

9. To observe some special occasion _____

10. A message transmitted by telegraph _____

11. A word for love _____

12. One of the planets _____

13. At the same time _____

14. To permit _____

15. An animal that hoots _____

WORD STAIR PUZZLE

Use the clues to fill in the grid.

1. 10 - 9 = _____

2. What you hear with

3. Follow the yellow brick _____

4. To call a number on the phone

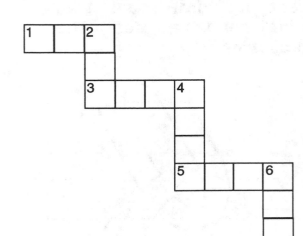
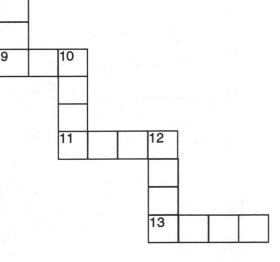

5. To see

6. An Australian animal

7. The space something occupies

8. Almost

9. 2,000 pounds

10. Hammer and _____

11. _____ Erie

12. Border

13. What a hen lays

COMPETITIVE WORD CHAIN

To play, two or more players start at the same time. The object is to fill in all the blanks with a three-, four-, or five-letter word, depending on the number of blanks given. Each word must begin with the last letter of the preceding word. The first word may start with any letter. (Words may not be repeated.) The first player to complete all the words wins.

1. ___ ___ ___

2. ___ ___ ___ ___

3. ___ ___ ___ ___ ___

4. ___ ___ ___ ___

5. ___ ___ ___

6. ___ ___ ___ ___

7. ___ ___ ___ ___ ___

8. ___ ___ ___ ___

9. ___ ___ ___

10. ___ ___ ___ ___

11. ___ ___ ___ ___ ___

12. ___ ___ ___ ___

13. ___ ___ ___

14. ___ ___ ___ ___

15. ___ ___ ___ ___ ___

16. ___ ___ ___ ___

17. ___ ___ ___

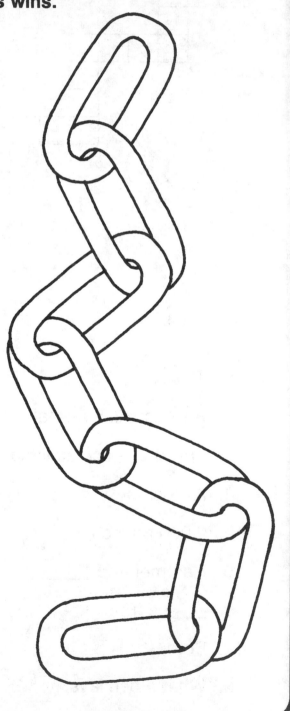

RE"CON"STRUCT THESE WORDS

Each phrase below is a clue for a word that contains the letters CON.

1. U.S. state whose capital is Hartford _____

2. Woman's name _____

3. The end _____

4. Seasonings for food _____

5. To hide_____

6. To go on _____

7. To extend good wishes _____

8. Mixed up _____

9. To make up _____

10. A musical entertainment _____

11. Letters other than vowels _____

12. The seven main land masses on Earth _____

13. To become friends again_____

14. Strong building material _____

15. Bits of colored paper thrown at celebrations _____

CAR WORD PARTS

Each word or phrase below is a clue for a word that contains the letters CAR.

1. Saturday morning television shows _____

2. Kind of candy _____

3. Major league team _____

4. Box _____

5. Traveling show _____

6. Flower _____

7. Floor covering _____

8. Animals that feed chiefly on meat _____

9. Unit of weight for precious stones _____

10. A merry-go-round _____

11. Part of the engine of a car _____

12. To get rid of _____

13. Type of sweater Mr. Rogers wears _____

14. A picture that exaggerates a person's features _____

15. To imprison _____

NO! NO! A THOUSAND TIMES NO!

Each phrase below is a clue for a word that contains the letters NO.

1. No person _____

2. City in Tennessee _____

3. Rap on the door _____

4. Wanderer_____

5. Range of information a person has_____

6. Lengthy story _____

7. Sound _____

8. The Biblical man who built an ark _____

9. Either of the two times each year when day and night are of equal length_____

10. A pig's nose, mouth, and jaws _____

11. Small, elf-like, imaginary being _____

12. A loop with a slip knot that tightens as the rope is pulled _____

13. Foolishness_____

14. Body part used for smelling _____

15. A macaroni-like food made in flat strips _____

IT'S THE CAT'S MEOW

Each word or phrase below is a clue for a word that contains the letters CAT.

1. Baseball position _____

2. Condiment _____

3. To make more of _____

4. Prescription drug _____

5. Scram! _____

6. Underground burial sites _____

7. Time off _____

8. Religion _____

9. Career _____

10. Mimic _____

11. 10-event contest _____

12. Faithful _____

13. Beef or dairy _____

14. To teach _____

15. Disaster _____

WHAT DOES IT MEAN?

Explain the meaning of each word or phrase below.

1. Oodles _____

2. Black sheep _____

3. Etc. _____

4. Ballpark figure _____

5. Pet peeve _____

6. Vamoose _____

7. S.O.S. _____

8. White elephant gift _____

9. Vice versa _____

10. Okey-dokey _____

11. Sign your John Hancock _____

12. Bone to pick _____

13. Southpaw _____

14. Backseat driver _____

15. Once in a blue moon _____

HIDDEN ANIMALS

Hidden in each sentence is the name of an animal. Each can be found either in the middle of a word or by combining the end of one word with the beginning of the next. Circle or underline the animal name in each sentence.

1. Eric owns his own computer store.

2. Is Mr. Roy Sterwin our new teacher?

3. Try some of these green grapes.

4. Sarah entered the building from the back door.

5. Sheryl, I only have 25 cents in my pocket.

6. The teacher made Ernie stay after school to get his work made up.

7. We will leave for the picnic at 11:45.

8. Please allow me to introduce you.

9. She cannot stand to be around people who smoke.

10. I can go at 7:30

A PUZZLING PROVERB

Fill in the answers to the following clues. Then, transfer the letters to the corresponding numbered blanks to reveal a famous proverb.

1. If the capital of Hawaii is Honolulu, circle P. If not, circle O.

2. If there are five rings on the Olympic flag, circle O. If there are six, circle A.

3. If an insect has eight legs, circle T. If not, circle W.

4. If the result of two numbers added together is called the sum, circle C. If not, circle N.

5. If 131 is a numerical palindrome, circle F. If not, circle H.

6. If there are 13 in a baker's dozen, circle T. If not, circle D.

7. If antonyms mean the opposite, circle Y. If not, circle N.

8. If a comma is used in a contraction, circle N. If not, circle T.

9. If a name for low clouds is fog, circle R. If it is not, circle A.

10. If an eight-sided figure is called an octagon, circle A. If not, circle M.

11. If a baby kangaroo is a kid, circle Y. If it is a joey, circle M.

12. If Washington is one of the four presidents carved on Mt. Rushmore, circle U. If not, circle H.

13. If your mother's sister is your grandmother, circle H. If not, circle N.

14. If 2,000 pounds equals one ton, circle H. If not, circle F.

___ ___ ___ , ___ ___ ___ ___
 6   2   13   8

___ ___ ___ until
 2   5   5

___ ___ ___   ___ ___ ___ ___ ___
 8   2   11   2   9   9   2   3

___ ___ ___ ___   ___ ___ ___
 3   14 10   8   7   2   12

___ ___ ___   ___ ___   ___ ___ ___ ___ ___
 4   10 13   6   2   8   2   6   10   7

AROUND AND AROUND YOU GO

Starting with the letter "D," write every third letter written around the picture on the lines below. The result will be a famous proverb.

Ⓓ D T O O O R N D R T A O P

Do __ ' __ ___ ___ _____

_____ , _____

_____ __ _____

DECODE SCHOOL SUPPLIES AND STATES

Each group of letters below is a list of related names in code. Each group has its own code. Brainstorm some names to fit each category. Once you have identified a name, use the known letters to decode the other names. (One letter of the first group has been done for you.)

School Supplies

1. AIFOA _____   A = R

2. CVVDL _____

3. BHBOA _____

4. JFIO _____

5. EVMOCVVDL _____

6. BOEGNFL _____

7. NED BOE _____

8. GAHRVEL _____

9. LMHBFOA _____

10. KHAQOAL _____

States

1. IHGGHOOHH _____

2. GHXPDOLD _____

3. DFDXDWD _____

4. OAZIC VDLAID _____

5. ACJA _____

6. YFAPJVD _____

7. JFFJGAJO _____

8. GHK WHSJBA _____

9. CDKDJJ _____

10. BDFJYAPGJD _____

GRANDPARENT'S DAY

There are at least 50 words (of 3 letters or more) hidden in the words "Grandparent's Day." Can you find them? If you run out of room, use the back side of this page.

1. _____
2. _____
3. _____
4. _____
5. _____
6. _____
7. _____
8. _____
9. _____
10. _____
11. _____
12. _____
13. _____
14. _____
15. _____
16. _____
17. _____
18. _____
19. _____
20. _____
21. _____
22. _____
23. _____
24. _____
26. _____
27. _____
28. _____
29. _____
30. _____
31. _____
32. _____
33. _____
34. _____
35. _____
36. _____
37. _____
38. _____
39. _____
40. _____
41. _____
42. _____
43. _____
44. _____
45. _____
46. _____
47. _____
48. _____
49. _____

FOUR-LETTER WORDS

Below are listed the middle letters of some four-letter words.
Fill in the blanks to make four-letter words.

___ a n ___	___ i d ___
___ e a ___	___ o v ___
___ a r ___	___ a i ___
___ e l ___	___ a m ___
___ o a ___	___ f a ___
___ i k ___	___ a v ___
___ o l ___	___ o r ___
___ a r ___	___ v e ___
___ o u ___	___ y p ___
___ o o ___	___ a s ___

Here are the initial and final letters of some four-letter words.
Fill in the blanks to make four-letter words.

c ___ ___ t	b ___ ___ d
s ___ ___ t	m ___ ___ t
d ___ ___ e	t ___ ___ e
r ___ ___ n	p ___ ___ t
l ___ ___ d	b ___ ___ t
f ___ ___ d	h ___ ___ e
s ___ ___ d	d ___ ___ r
s ___ ___ r	e ___ ___ n
a ___ ___ e	g ___ ___ e
h ___ ___ t	m ___ ___ t

DOUBLE LETTERS

Each word or phrase below is a clue for a word that contains consecutive double letters.

1. Someone who tosses trash in public areas _____

2. Greeting _____

3. Joyful _____

4. To eat hurriedly _____

5. Not easy _____

6. Small pool of water _____

7. Awful _____

8. Duck _____

9. Farewell _____

10. Large monkey _____

11. Cushion for the head _____

12. To talk a lot and quickly _____

13. Opposite of defense _____

14. Elk _____

15. Designation where an envelope should be sent_____

BEGIN AND END

Each phrase below is a clue for an answer that begins and ends with the same letter.

1. Child's sidewalk game _____

2. A continent _____

3. Songs sung alone _____

4. A majestic bird _____

5. A type of boat _____

6. Rudolph _____

7. One of the sense organs _____

8. A common man's name _____

9. To quiet down _____

10. Blue-green color _____

11. A young bird's noise _____

12. Midday _____

13. Old-fashioned type of margarine _____

14. The hardest mineral _____

15. The day before today _____

ANIMALS ANIMALS EVERYWHERE

Using the letters of the alphabet, A through Z, brainstorm a list of animals. Then, try to start a second list.

A _____

B _____

C _____

D _____

E _____

F _____

G _____

H _____

I _____

J _____

K _____

L _____

M _____

N _____

O _____

P _____

Q _____

R _____

S _____

T _____

U _____

V _____

W _____

X _____

Y _____

Z _____

ABCDEFG

How many words can you spell using only the first seven letters of the alphabet? The letters may be used more than one time within a word.

_____   _____

_____   _____

_____   _____

_____   _____

_____   _____

_____   _____

_____   _____

_____   _____

_____   _____

_____   _____

_____   _____

_____   _____

BACK TO SCHOOL

List words related to school that begin with each letter of the alphabet. Then, try to start a second list.

A _____

B _____

C _____

D _____

E _____

F _____

G _____

H _____

I _____

J _____

K _____

L _____

M _____

N _____

O _____

P _____

Q _____

R _____

S _____

T _____

U _____

V _____

W _____

X _____

Y _____

Z _____

ANAGRAMS

Reorder the letters of each word below to make a new word.

1. ocean _____

2. snap _____

3. Brian _____

4. owl _____

5. melon _____

6. pots _____

7. flea _____

8. ring _____

9. art _____

10. gum _____

11. heart _____

12. bat _____

13. paws _____

14. ape _____

15. tone _____

16. tap _____

17. stop _____

18. not _____

19. pore _____

20. wee _____

COMPOUND WORDS

Write a word in the blank between each set of words. The trick is that the new word must complete a compound word both to the left and to the right of it. The first one has been done for you.

1. dug _____out_____ side

2. foot _____ ladder

3. arrow _____ line

4. country _____ walk

5. tea _____ belly

6. camp _____ place

7. basket _____ room

8. touch _____ stairs

9. drug _____ keeper

10. base _____ room

11. flash _____ house

12. hill _____ walk

13. look _____ doors

14. quarter _____ bone

15. some _____ ever

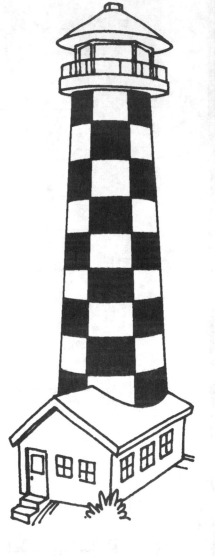

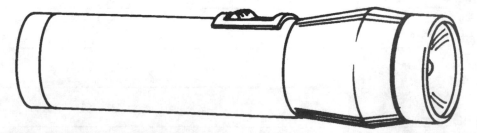

PROVERBS

Add the missing vowels to complete these famous proverbs.

1. __ __ r l __ t __ b __ d __ __ __ r l __
   t __ r __ s __ , m __ k __ s __ m __ n
   h __ __ l t h __ , w __ __ l t h __ , __ n d
   w __ s __ .

2. __ n __ p p l __ __ d __ y k __ __ p s
   t h __ d __ c t __ r __ w __ __

3. __ s t __ t c h __ n t __ m __ s __ v __ s
   n __ n __ .

4. B __ t t __ r l __ t __ t h __ n n __ v __ r.

5. D __ n't c __ __ n t y __ __ r c h __ c k __ n s
   b __ f __ r __ t h __ y h __ t c h.

6. D __ n't p __ t __ l l y __ __ r __ g g s __ n
   __ n __ b __ s k __ t.

7. L __ __ k b __ f __ r e y __ __ l __ __ p.

8. H __ s t __ m __ k __ s w __ s t __ .

9. W h __ t __ v __ r __ s w __ r t h d __ __ __ n g,
   __ s w __ r t h d __ __ __ n g w __ l l.

10. A __ __ t h __ g l __ t t __ r s __ s
    n __ t g __ l d.

SIX-LETTER WORDS

Below are 46 boxes. Each box contains either the first or last half of a six-letter word. Can you match first and last halves to form 23 words? You may wish to cut out the boxes.

yel–	son–	–tle	–cil
win–	gal–	–fee	–ple
sam–	pay–	–her	–low
bat–	car–	–mer	–day
lit–	sum–	–net	–bol
sym–	vio–	–try	–tle
jun–	win–	–way	–let
bet–	pen–	–ior	–day
ham–	any–	–ner	–ter
tri–	mid–	–ter	–pod
–gop	cof–	–lop	–mer
let–			–ton

WHICH WORD SHALL I USE?

Circle the correct word on the right that matches the word or phrase on the left.

1. story   tale/tail

2. rabbit   hare/hair

3. bus token   fair/fare

4. odor   sent/scent

5. make a purchase   buy/by/bye

6. one   lone/loan

7. also   to/two/too

8. assistant   aid/aide

9. land by a lake   beach/beech

10. two   pare/pair

11. large   great/grate

12. change   alter/altar

13. atmosphere   air/heir

14. grief   mourning/morning

15. land   aisle/isle

SYNONYMS, ANTONYMS, HOMOPHONES

Identify each pair of words as synonyms (S), antonyms (A), or homophones (H).

1. _____ near—far

2. _____ desire—want

3. _____ foe—friend

4. _____ close—near

5. _____ led—lead

6. _____ genuine—real

7. _____ healthy—sick

8. _____ maid—made

9. _____ hurry—rush

10. _____ meat—meet

11. _____ wide—narrow

12. _____ limp—slack

13. _____ clear—plain

14. _____ strong—weak

15. _____ none—nun

16. _____ mix—blend

17. _____ pale—pail

18. _____ often—seldom

SIMILES

A simile is a figure of speech in which two things are compared with the words like or as, such as in "He moved as quick as a wink." Complete the following similes.

1. As blind as _____

2. As cool as _____

3. As mad as _____

4. As happy as _____

5. As busy as _____

6. As neat as _____

7. As flat as _____

8. As pale as _____

9. As easy as _____

10. As proud as _____

11. As fresh as _____

12. As hard as _____

13. As light as _____

14. As sharp as _____

15. As wise as _____

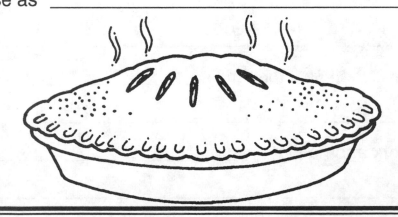

PROVERBS

Proverbs are old, familiar sayings that often give advice for daily living. Complete each of the following proverbs and explain what they mean.

1. Early to bed and early to rise, _____

   _____

2. Don't count your chickens _____

   _____

3. Birds of a feather _____

   _____

4. A penny saved _____

   _____

5. Two wrongs _____

   _____

6. When the cat's away, _____

   _____

7. Look before _____

   _____

8. Never look a gift horse _____

   _____

9. Never put off until tomorrow _____

   _____

10. All work and no play _____

    _____

ANALOGIES

Analogies are comparisons. Complete each analogy below. An example has been done for you.

Ear is to hearing as eye is to sight.

1. Cardinals is to St. Louis as Dodgers is to _____

2. A.M. is to before noon as P.M. is to _____

3. Three is to triangle as eight is to_____

4. Tear is to tore as see is to _____

5. Springfield is to Illinois as Austin is to_____

6. Carpet is to floor as bedspread is to _____

7. Go is to green as stop is to_____

8. Purple is to grapes as red is to _____

9. Ghost is to Halloween as bunny is to_____

10. Son is to dad as daughter is to _____

11. Jelly is to toast as syrup is to _____

12. Ear is to hear as eye is to _____

13. Oink is to pig as cluck is to _____

14. Mississippi is to U.S. as Nile is to _____

15. Clock is to time as thermometer is to _____

16. V is to 5 as C is to _____

17. Up is to down as ceiling is to _____

18. Car is to driver as plane is to _____

19. Sleep is to tired as eat is to _____

20. Bird is to nest as bee is to _____

COMPLETE THE PHRASE

1. Stop, drop, and _____

2. Ready, set, _____

3. Knife, fork, and _____

4. Morning, noon, and _____

5. Snap, crackle, and _____

6. Up, up, and _____

7. The butcher, the baker, and the _____

8. A hop, a skip, and _____

9. Red, white, and _____

10. Stop, look, and _____

11. Bacon, lettuce, and _____

12. Red, yellow, and _____

13. Men, women, and _____

14. Healthy, wealthy, and _____

15. Go, fight, _____

16. Coffee, tea, or _____

17. Tall, dark, and _____

18. Sun, moon, and _____

74

WHAT IS IT?

Check the correct box for each location on the chart.

	City	State/Province	Country	Continent
1. Mexico				
2. Montreal				
3. Lima				
4. Africa				
5. Reno				
6. North America				
7. Alberta				
8. Germany				
9. Quebec				
10. Oklahoma				
11. Europe				
12. Los Angeles				
13. Switzerland				
14. Illinois				
15. Australia				
16. Canada				
17. Asia				
18. Budapest				
19. Maine				
20. Italy				

ANSWER KEY

Page 3
1. Stimpy
2. Gretel
3. Lois Lane
4. Beauty
5. Batman
6. Mickey
7. Ken
8. Wilbur
9. Olive Oyl
10. Kermit
11. Punch
12. Dr. Jeckell
13. Jill
14. the Tramp
15. Ernie

Page 4
Answers will vary. Here are some examples.
mittens
gloves
socks
shoes
sandals
slippers
ice skates
roller skates
skis
boots
shoelaces
jeans
shorts
pajamas
earrings
glasses
pliers
binoculars
scissors
dice

Page 5
Answers will vary. Here are some examples.
bowling ball
donut
Lifesaver candy
your nose
pencil sharpener
salt shaker
basketball hoop
funnel
strainer
bagel
Swiss cheese
ring
arm band
light bulb socket
straw
macaroni
honeycomb
miniature golf course
computer paper
handcuffs
needle
paper punch

Page 6
Answers will vary.

Page 7
1. Adams, Jefferson, and Madison
2. Lincoln, Jefferson, and Washington
3. the cowardly lion, the tin man, and the scarecrow
4. Papa, Mama, and Baby
5. red, yellow, and blue
6. Flora, Fauna, and Merriwether
7. the butcher, the baker, and the candlestick maker

8. Casper, Melchior, and Balthasar
9. reading, 'riting, and 'rithmetic
10. Huey, Dewey, and Louie
11. Curly, Moe, and Larry
12. Mizaru, Mikazaur, and Mazaru

Page 8
1. cardinal directions
2. female relatives
3. odd numbers
4. words for pretty
5. continents
6. months (or months with thirty days)
7. states in the U.S.
8. astronauts
9. boy's names starting with P
10. planets
11. flowers
12. things that have three of something
13. some of the Seven Dwarfs
14. primary colors
15. reference books

Page 9
Accept all reasonable answers. These are the most likely.
1. cold
2. key
3. white (or blue)
4. soul
5. holler
6. right
7. eggs
8. mouse
9. down
10. fries
11. quiet
12. lightning
13. forth
14. thin
15. nails
16. stones
17. pains
18. butter
19. nails
20. seek

Page 10
Laura: koala and hamburger
Phil: zebra and hot dog
Jane: giraffe and popcorn
Mike: monkey and corndog

Page 11
Andrea: July 10
Andrew: February 15
Sarah: May 1
Sam: March 24
Jill: December 25
Jeff: October 15
Millie: April 1
Max: September 9

Page 12
Nicole: flute for 40 minutes
Sean: drums for 30 minutes
Justin: clarinet for 35 minutes
Janis: piano for 45 minutes

Page 13
Matt: baseball
Brian: basketball
Jon: soccer
Neil: tennis
Jason: hockey

Page 14
Chelsea: B
Linda: C-
Marcia: A
Morgan: C
Casie: D

Page 15
A.J. Smith is 8.
Andy Jones is 9.
Andrew Rogers is 10.

Page 16
Cross out all letters but A, H, K, N, R, S, and U. The remaining letters, when read in order, spell, "a shrunk skunk."

Page 17

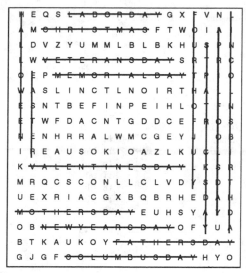

Page 18

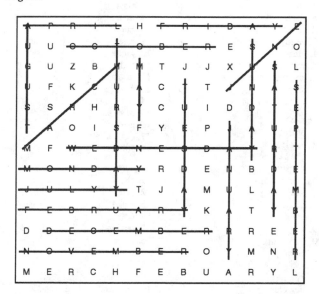

Page 19
Responses will vary.

Page 20
Answers will vary.

Page 21
Answers will vary.

Page 22
Answers will vary.

Page 23
1. Open up!
2. You're under arrest.
3. double cross

4. I understand.
5. a hole in one
6. Holy cow!
7. all mixed up
8. tricycle
9. Good afternoon.
10. Big Mac
11. highchair
12. touchdown

Page 24
1. Jack-in-the-box
2. Tiny Tim
3. pair of dice
4. long underwear
5. reading between the lines
6. Get up!
7. just in time
8. G.I. overseas
9. going on a diet
10. sandbox
11. downtown
12. man in the moon

Page 25
1. $6 + 4 - 1 - 2 + 6 + 2 = 15$
2. $9 + 1 - 3 + 1 - 4 + 1 = 5$
3. $9 - 3 + 4 - 1 + 2 + 3 = 14$
4. $5 - 1 + 1 + 3 + 4 + 6 = 18$
5. $9 - 8 + 6 + 3 - 5 + 3 = 8$
6. $2 - 1 + 8 + 9 - 3 + 5 = 20$
7. $5 + 3 + 2 - 4 + 1 + 5 = 12$
8. $4 + 9 + 3 - 7 + 3 - 1 = 11$
9. $7 - 6 + 2 + 8 - 7 - 1 = 3$
10. $9 + 9 - 9 + 2 - 2 - 8 = 1$

Page 26
1. sight, sound, smell, taste, and touch
2. Papa, Mama, and Baby
3. red, orange, yellow, green, blue, indigo, and violet
4. reading, 'riting, and 'rithmetic
5. Dasher, Dancer, Prancer, Vixen, Comet, Cupid, Donner, Blitzen, and Rudolph
6. Erie, Michigan, Superior, Huron, and Ontario
7. April, June, September, and November
8. blue, yellow, and red
9. red and white
10. Happy, Sleepy, Doc, Grumpy, Bashful, Sneezey, and Dopey

Page 27
Answers will vary.

Page 28
Time Span
1. second
2. minute
3. hour
4. day
5. week
6. fortnight
7. month
8. year
9. decade
10. score
11. century
12. millennium

How Long Is It?
1. 1000 milliseconds
2. 60 seconds
3. 60 minutes
4. 24 hours
5. 7 days
6. 2 weeks
7. 28 to 31 days
8. 12 months
9. 10 years
10. 20 years
11. 100 years
12. 1000 years

Page 29
1. loose
2. globe
3. bees
4. oil
5. hose
6. ill
7. boohoo
8. Bill
9. Boise
10. big

Page 30
1. 7 dwarfs in *Snow White*
2. 9 players on a baseball team
3. 5 lakes in the Great Lakes
4. 60 seconds in a minute
5. 12 inches in a foot
6. 32 teeth in an adult
7. 7 days in a week
8. 3 sides in a triangle
9. 7 continents on the Earth
10. 12 months in a year
11. 9 planets in the Solar System
12. 100 pennies in a dollar
13. 11 players on a football team
14. 24 hours in a day
15. 12 eggs in a dozen
16. 4 seasons in a year
17. 50 states in the United States
18. 3 primary colors
19. 13 stripes on the U.S. flag
20. 7 colors in a rainbow

Page 31
1. 4
2. 100
3. 3
4. 10
5. 365
6. 7
7. 12
8. 6
9. 50
10. 5
11. 6
12. 121
13. 64
14. 6
15. 24

Page 32
1. 2
2. 5
3. 50
4. 4
5. 88
6. 5
7. 5
8. 3
9. 7
10. 12
11. 1
12. 9
13. 64
14. 100
15. 66

Page 33
1. T
2. T
3. F
4. F
5. T
6. T
7. T
8. F
9. T
10. F

11. F
12. T
13. T
14. T
15. F
16. F
17. F
18. T

Page 34
1. the rear plate
2. 30
3. red
4. Thomas Jefferson
5. balls
6. right
7. 6
8. 90 degrees
9. 5 or 9
10. 8
11. denominator
12. autumn or fall
13. left
14. maximum

Page 35
1. T
2. F
3. T
4. F
5. F
6. T
7. F
8. T
9. F
10. T
11. T
12. T
13. F
14. T
15. T
16. T
17. F
18. F

Page 36
1. subject and predicate
2. an apostrophe
3. nouns
4. fiction
5. Templeton
6. comma
7. an opinion
8. a comma
9. won't
10. a glossary
11. sheep
12. opposite
13. maybe
14. a fable
15. haiku

Page 37
1. thermometer
2. invertebrates
3. gills
4. oysters
5. telescope
6. Saturn
7. a skunk
8. 8
9. hummingbird
10. fog
11. a tadpole
12. bats
13. a school
14. toadstool
15. poles

Page 38

1. 120
2. 10
3. a triangle
4. tell time
5. 4,000
6. a colon
7. 12
8. 6
9. sum
10. 100
11. 6
12. octagon
13. 6
14. 10
15. 24

Page 39
1. North America
2. east
3. red
4. Mississippi
5. north
6. Alexander Graham Bell
7. atlas
8. Mt. Everest
9. island
10. Pinta, Niña, and Santa Maria
11. Mt. Rushmore
12. Huron, Ontario, Michigan, Erie, and Superior
13. Peru
14. Pacific
15. Honolulu

Page 40
1. 6
2. Lincoln
3. buffalo
4. red/yellow
5. peacock
6. captain
7. autumn
8. sheep
9. Dopey
10. yellow
11. glasses
12. your uncle
13. origami
14. joey
15. white

Page 41
1. ill Bill
2. bad lad
3. glum chum
4. shy fly
5. funny bunny
6. plump ump
7. fat cat
8. sad dad
9. wet pet
10. pink drink
11. big pig
12. lazy daisy
13. wee flea
14. sick chick
15. fat rat

Page 42
Answers will vary.

Page 43
1. North
2. Street or Saint
3. railroad
4. South America
5. Master of Ceremonies
6. cash on delivery
7. Wednesday
8. before noon

9. chapter
10. dozen
11. quart
12. package
13. maximum
14. Avenue
15. September
16. year
17. building
18. number
19. temperature
20. post office

Page 44
1. gold
2. bold
3. bolt
4. colt
5. molt
6. mole
7. hole
8. hold
9. mold
10. mild
11. wild
12. wilt
13. will
14. wall
15. ball
16. call
17. fall
18. fill
19. file
20. pile

Page 45
1. bathe
2. happy
3. early
4. horse
5. motor
6. boat
7. instantly
8. buck
9. release
10. globe
11. fight
12. luggage
13. desire
14. combine
15. pest
16. crow
17. outlaw
18. July

Page 46
1. chew
2. ewe
3. weed
4. edible
5. letter
6. erase
7. season
8. once
9. celebrate
10. telegram
11. amour
12. Uranus
13. usual
14. allow
15. owl

#TCM 488 Brain Teasers—Grade 3   78   ©*1995 Teacher Created Materials, Inc.*

Page 47
1. one
2. ear
3. road
4. dial
5. look
6. koala
7. area
8. about
9. ton
10. nail
11. lake
12. edge
13. eggs

Page 48
Answers will vary.

Page 49
1. Connecticut
2. Connie
3. conclusion
4. condiments
5. conceal
6. continue
7. congratulations
8. confused
9. concoct
10. concert
11. consonants
12. continents
13. reconcile
14. concrete
15. confetti

Page 50
1. cartoons
2. caramel
3. Cardinals
4. carton
5. carnival
6. carnation
7. carpet
8. carnivores
9. carat
10. carousel
11. carburetor
12. discard
13. cardigan
14. caricature
15. incarcerate

Page 51
1. nobody
2. Knoxville
3. knock
4. nomad
5. knowledge
6. novel
7. noise
8. Noah
9. equinox
10. snout
11. gnome
12. noose
13. nonsense
14. nose
15. noodles

Page 52
1. catcher
2. catsup
3. duplicate
4. medication
5. scat
6. catacombs
7. vacation
8. Catholicism
9. vocation
10. copycat
11. decathlon
12. dedicated
13. cattle
14. educate
15. catastrophe

Page 53
1. an abundance of
2. a tarnished member of a respectable family
3. and so on
4. somewhere around this amount
5. an aggravation
6. Leave.
7. Help!
8. item with very little or no value
9. the other way around
10. Agreed.
11. sign your name
12. issue to discuss or complain about
13. left-handed
14. someone tells the driver how to drive
15. not very often

Page 54
1. cow
2. oyster
3. ape
4. hen
5. lion
6. deer
7. cat
8. seal
9. bear
10. goat

Pages 55–56
Don't put off until tomorrow what you can do today.

Page 57
School Supplies
1. ruler
2. books
3. paper
4. glue
5. notebooks
6. pencils
7. ink pen
8. crayons
9. stapler
10. markers

States
1. Tennessee
2. Nebraska
3. Alabama
4. South Dakota
5. Ohio
6. Florida
7. Illinois
8. New Mexico
9. Hawaii
10. California

Page 58
Answers will vary.

Page 59
Answers will vary.

Page 60
1. litterbug
2. hello
3. happy
4. gobble
5. difficult
6. puddle
7. terrible
8. mallard
9. good-bye
10. baboon
11. pillow
12. chatter
13. offense
14. moose
15. address

Page 61
1. hopscotch
2. Asia
3. solos
4. eagle
5. kayak
6. reindeer
7. eye
8. Bob
9. hush
10. aqua
11. peep
12. noon
13. oleo
14. diamond
15. yesterday

Page 62
Answers will vary. Here is one example.
alligator
buffalo
crocodile
donkey
elephant
fox
guinea pig
hippopotamus
ibex
jackal
kitten
lion
mouse
nightingale
owl
pig
quail
rattlesnake
shark
tiger
unicorn
vixen
whippoorwill
xantho
yellowhammer
zebra

Page 63
Answers will vary. Here are some examples.
age
ace
bad
badge
bade
bag
babe
bead
bed
bee
beg
cabbage
cafe
cage
cad
cab
deed
deaf
egg
edge
face
fad
fade
fed
gab
gag

Page 64
Answers will vary. Here is one example.
administrator
books
chalk
drinking fountain
eraser
files
globe
homework
industrious
jumprope
knowledge
library
music
notes
open house
principal
quiet
recess
students
teacher
understanding
video
world history
xylophone
yard
zeal

Page 65
Answers will vary. Here is one example for each.
1. ocean — canoe
2. snap — pans
3. Brian — brain
4. owl — low
5. melon — lemon
6. pots — stop
7. flea — leaf
8. ring — grin
9. art — tar
10. gum — mug
11. heart — Earth
12. bat — tab
13. paws — wasp
14. ape — pea
15. tone — note
16. tap — pat
17. stop — pots
18. not — ton
19. pore — rope
20. wee — ewe

Page 66
1. out
2. step
3. head
4. side
5. pot
6. fire
7. ball
8. down
9. store
10. ball
11. light
12. side
13. out
14. back
15. how

Page 67
1. Early to bed and early to rise, makes a man healthy, wealthy, and wise.
2. An apple a day deeps the doctor away.
3. A stitch in time saves nine.
4. Better late than never.
5. Don't count your chickens before they hatch.
6. Don't put all your eggs in one basket.
7. Look before you leap.
8. Haste makes waste.
9. Whatever is worth doing, is worth doing well.
10. All that glitters is not gold.

Page 68
wintry
hammer
pencil
carton
little
sonnet
gopher
yellow
payday
battle
junior
letter
sample
violet
better
tripod
anyway
gallop
midday
coffee
winner
summer
symbol

Page 69
1. tale
2. hare
3. fare
4. scent
5. buy
6. lone
7. too
8. aide
9. beach
10. pair
11. great
12. alter
13. air
14. mourning
15. isle

Page 70
1. A
2. S
3. A
4. S
5. H
6. S
7. A
8. H
9. S
10. H
11. A
12. S
13. S
14. A
15. H
16. S
17. H
18. A

Page 71
1. a bat
2. a cucumber
3. a hornet
4. a lark
5. a bee
6. a pin
7. a pancake
8. a ghost
9. pie
10. a peacock
11. a daisy
12. a rock
13. a feather
14. a tack
15. an owl

Page 72
1. . . . makes a man healthy, wealthy, and wise.
2. . . before they hatch.
3. . . . . flock together.
4. . . . is a penny earned.
5. . . . don't make a right.
6. . . . the mice will play.
7. . . . you leap.
8. . . . in the mouth.
9. . . . what you can do today.
10. . . . .makes Jack a dull boy.

Page 73
Some answers may vary.
1. Los Angeles
2. after noon
3. octagon
4. saw
5. Texas
6. bed
7. red
8. cherries
9. Easter
10. mother
11. pancakes
12. see
13. chicken
14. Egypt
15. temperature
16. 100
17. floor
18. pilot
19. hungry
20. hive

Page 74
Some answers may vary.
1. roll
2. go
3. spoon
4. night
5. pop
6. away
7. candlestick maker
8. jump
9. blue
10. listen
11. tomato
12. green or blue
13. children
14. wise
15. win
16. milk
17. handsome
18. stars

Page 75
1. country
2. city
3. city
4. continent
5. city
6. continent
7. state/province
8. country
9. city
10. state/province
11. continent
12. city
13. country
14. state/province
15. continent
16. country
17. continent
18. city
19. state/province
20. country